Toon-Ups
for the Soul

TOON-UPS FOR THE SOUL

JOE McCORMICK

Evergreen
PRESS

ISBN 1-58169-161-0
For Worldwide Distribution
Printed in the U.S.A.

Evergreen Press
P.O. Box 191540
Mobile, AL 36619

FOREWORD

When Gary Larson quit doing his *Far Side* cartoons he left a void, at least in my house. My son Ross and I used to turn to his cartoons first in the daily newspaper. Ross was so impressed by *Far Side* that he drew a series of his own weird cartoons (two of which I include on the following pages). Ross might have become a cartoonist himself if he hadn't become a computer whiz. Many of my cartoons also show Larson's influence. (I hope to goodness I haven't accidentally duplicated any of them here!)

Our daughter Missy doesn't draw, but her sense of humor is great. For years her favorite Christmas gift from me was the latest Jerry Clower tape.

Coincidentally (or not?), I have to say that there has not been a lot of sickness in our household. Could be the Bible is right, and a good laugh is worth more in prevention than a handful of expensive pills are in cure.

Anyway, I'm a believer in that principle. I hope you are too, and that you will turn these pages slowly, get a chuckle from the cartoons, meditate on the scriptures, and find it all a delight and health to your bones.

Here's to your health!

—*Joe McCormick*

"SORRY, MR. SIMMONS, BUT YOUR POLICY ONLY COVERS <u>TOTAL</u> DISABILITY!"

CHICKEN HELL

Dedication

To Christine.
She gets my jokes.

*A merry heart
doeth good
like a medicine.*

Proverbs 17:22

© 2004

NOAH BOARDS THE ARK WITH ONE FINAL ITEM.

…The prudent man looketh well to his going.
Proverbs 14:15

MATERNITY WARD

FROM THE MOMENT OF HIS BIRTH, JAMAL'S CAREER PATH WAS VIRTUALLY ASSURED.

A man's gift maketh room for him,
and bringeth him before great men.
Proverbs 18:16

TELEMARKETERS KILLING TIME, WAITING FOR THE DINNER HOUR TO START WORK.

*He also that is slothful in his work
is brother to him that is a great waster.*
Proverbs 18:9

PASTOR NED SEEKS THE LORD'S WILL ABOUT
WHETHER HE SHOULD ACCEPT THE
CHURCH IN ORLANDO.

Delight thyself also in the Lord;
and he shall give thee the desires of thine heart.
Psalm 37:4

*Be sober, be vigilant; because your adversary
the devil, as a roaring lion, walketh about, seeking
whom he may devour:* 1 Peter 5:8

SIMMONS WAS ON THE THRESHOLD OF MAKING A
FORTUNE. HE HAD DEVELOPED A CHEMICAL
THAT WOULD DISSOLVE ANYTHING. IF ONLY HE
COULD FIGURE OUT HOW TO PACKAGE IT.

*But will God really dwell on earth? The heavens, even
the highest heaven, cannot contain you. How much
less this temple I have built!* 1 Kings 8:27

HOLY LAND SCAMS

...I was a stranger, and ye took me in.
Matthew 25:35

RALPHY WAS A LOT LIVELIER AFTER THEY HAD THE TUBES PUT IN HIS EARS.

He that hath ears to hear, let him hear.
Matthew 11:15

FEEDING TIME AT ROBIN HOOD'S HOUSE

As arrows are in the hand of a mighty man;
so are children of the youth.
Psalm 127:4

WELL AWARE OF THE MISSIONARIES' RULE OF
EATING WHATEVER IS SET BEFORE THEM LEST
THEY OFFEND THEIR HOSTS, MABINI GETS
RID OF LAST WEEK'S MEATLOAF.

*And into whatsoever city ye enter, and they receive you,
eat such things as are set before you.*
Luke 10:8

HANDEL'S MESSIAH
BECOMES HEIMLICH'S MANEUVER.

*Be merciful unto me, O God: for man would swallow
me up; he fighting daily oppresseth me.*
Psalm 56:1

"MOM! I FEEL ALL BETTER NOW!
IT'S A MIRACLE!"

*...and shall shew great signs and wonders;
insomuch that, if it were possible, they shall
deceive the very elect.* Matthew 24:24

"WE'D BETTER TAKE AWAY LITTLE DAVID'S BOW AND ARROW AND GIVE HIM THIS. HE CAN'T HURT ANYBODY WITH A SLINGSHOT."

So David prevailed over the Philistine with a sling and with a stone, and smote the Philistine, and slew him.
I Samuel 17:50

I SEE BY YOUR NOSE RING THAT
YOU ARE A CHRISTIAN!"

Wherefore by their fruits ye shall know them.
Matthew 7:20

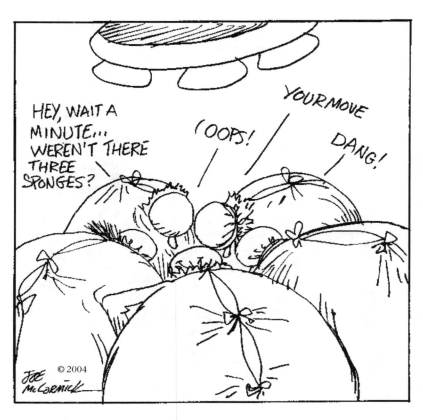

O.R. CHATTER...AS GOOD A REASON AS
ANY FOR PATIENT ANESTHESIA.

*See what they spew from their mouths--they spew out
swords from their lips, and they say, "Who can hear
us?"* Psalm 59:7 (NIV)

MYRTLE JOHANSEN, LONG-TIME FAD DIETER,
LOSES IT AT A WAL-MART DISPLAY AND
ENDS UP A HAPPY 911 EMERGENCY.

Wherefore do ye spend money for that which is not
bread? and your labour for that which satisfieth not?
hearken diligently unto me, and eat ye that which is
good, and let your soul delight itself in fatness. Isa. 55:2

AFTER THE FLOOD, NOAH BUILDS HIS FORTUNE ON THE SALE OF GARDEN FERTILIZER.

And God blessed Noah and his sons, and said unto them, Be fruitful, and multiply, and replenish the earth.
Genesis 9:1

PREHISTORIC PARKING LOTS

Your glorying is not good. Know ye not that a little leaven leaveneth the whole lump?
1 Corinthians 5:6

WHISTLER'S MOTHER FINALLY HAS ENOUGH.

In your patience possess ye your souls.
Luke 21:19

THE LEAP OF FAITH

For the wisdom of this world is foolishness with God.
For it is written, He taketh the wise in their own
craftiness. 1 Corinthians 3:19

SQUIRE DANNY CHANGED HIS MIND ABOUT SAILING
ON A PIRATE SHIP. AFTER GETTING A GOOD LOOK
AT THE CAPTAIN, HE DECIDED THE
GAIN WASN'T WORTH THE LOSS.

*For what shall it profit a man, if he shall
gain the whole world, and lose his own soul?*
Mark 8:36

"DRIVE ON, AGNES! HOW DO WE KNOW
WHAT HE HAS IN MIND?

Blessed are the merciful: for they shall obtain mercy.
Matthew 5:7

FINALLY PURVIS UNDERSTOOD WHY THE
MISSION HANDBOOK ADVISED AGAINST
SHAKING LEFT-HANDED WITH
THE BURINGIS.

A wise man's heart is at his right hand;
but a fool's heart at his left.
Ecclesiastes 10:2

Let your moderation be known unto all men.
Philippians 4:5

THE MARSHALL ARTIST

So God created man in his own image, in the image of God created he him; male and female created he them.
Genesis 1:27

OUR MISSIONARY FROM UPPER ZORGOVIA,
DESPERATE TO RETURN HOME FOR HIS
SCHEDULED FURLOUGH DURING THE AIRLINE
STRIKES, LOSES HIS LIFE IN A
RASH EXPERIMENT.

For ye shall not go out with haste...
Isaiah 52:12

THE COMPETITION GETS MORE
FIERCE EVERY YEAR.

And the tongue is a fire, a world of iniquity...
James 3:6

"HONEY, WE'RE EITHER GOING TO HAVE TO
GET RID OF THE DOG OR SELL THIS HOUSE!"

When goods increase, they are increased that eat them.
Ecclesiastes 5:11

ACTUALLY MOSES DIDN'T START STUTTERING UNTIL HIS SHEPHERD'S STAFF TURNED INTO A SNAKE.

And Moses said unto the Lord, O my Lord...I am slow of speech, and of a slow tongue.
Exodus 4:10

"FENWICK, I WISH YOU'D STOP REFERRING TO THAT CROCODILE-INFESTED SWAMP WE WENT THROUGH AS THE FIRST 'LEG' OF THE JOURNEY!"

Let no corrupt communication proceed out of your mouth, but that which is good to the use of edifying, that it may minister grace unto the hearers. Eph. 4:29

"DEAR, MAYBE WE SHOULD HAVE GONE AHEAD
AND LET TIMMIE GO SURFING TODAY
INSTEAD OF MAKING HIM MOW THE LAWN..."

Chasten thy son while there is hope,
and let not thy soul spare for his crying.
1 Proverbs 19:18

NEHI-A-MIAH LOSES HIS DISTINCTION
AS THE SHORTEST MAN MENTIONED IN
THE BIBLE WHEN BILDAD THE
SHU-HITE SHOWS UP.

For all have sinned, and come short of the glory of God.
Romans 3:23

"I THINK I JUST FOUND OUT WHY THEY'RE
NOT DOING ANY MORE MOON SHOTS...
THEY ALREADY BROUGHT
MOST OF IT BACK."

When I was a child, I spake as a child...
I Corinthians 13:11

"I'M AFRAID THE NEWS JUST KEEPS GETTING WORSE, MR. MODO. YOU ALSO NEED CORRECTIVE SHOES!"

Afterward Jesus findeth him in the temple, and said unto him, Behold, thou art made whole: sin no more, lest a worse thing come unto thee. John 5:14

"NOW LET ME GET THIS STRAIGHT, PROFESSOR...YOU CLAIM TO HAVE SUCCESSFULLY DEMONSTRATED HOW THE 'BIG BANG' ACTUALLY HAPPENED?"

In the beginning God created the heaven and the earth.
Genesis 1:1

A merry heart doeth good like a medicine:
but a broken spirit drieth the bones.
Proverbs 17:22

**"HEY, CHARLIE...THOSE POLICE DOGS ARE
BACK, AND THEY'RE CREEPIN' ME OUT!"**

*...the dogs eat of the crumbs which fall
from their masters' table.*
Matthew 15:27

"RITES, YOU IDIOT! I SAID, 'READ HIM THE LAST RITES!'"

And the prayer of faith shall save the sick, and the Lord shall raise him up; and if he have committed sins, they shall be forgiven him. James 5:15

"OH, HONEY, CAN WE BUY HIM? HE'S SMALL
ENOUGH FOR OUR APARTMENT,
AND HE'S SO CUTE!"

It is like a grain of mustard seed, which, when it is
sown in the earth, is less than all the seeds that be in
the earth: But when it is sown, it groweth up....
Mark 4:31-32

TIM DISCOVERS THAT TWO BEERS
CAN DISTORT ONE'S PERCEPTION MORE
THAN ONE MIGHT THINK.

*Wine is a mocker, strong drink is raging: and
whosoever is deceived thereby is not wise.*
Proverbs 20:1

© 2004

JOE M. CORMICK

AS THE YEARS PASSED, CEDRIC BECAME A SHADOW OF HIS FARMER SELF.

...our days on the earth are as a shadow,
and there is none abiding.
1 Chronicles 29:15b

"NOT *THAT* AGAIN?"

And having food and raiment let
us be therewith content.
1 Timothy 6:8

THE BISHOP'S WIFE HAD WARNED HIM THAT
TELLING ELEPHANT JOKES FROM THE PULPIT
WOULD ONE DAY GET HIM IN TROUBLE.

...and a prudent wife is from the Lord.
Proverbs 19:14b

IT WAS HAPPENING WITH ALARMING
FREQUENCY IN RESTAURANTS ACROSS THE
COUNTRY, PUTTING A SEVERE STRAIN
ON RESCUE AGENCIES.

*The righteous cry, and the Lord heareth, and delivereth
them out of all their troubles.*
Psalm 34:17

THE TARDY BIRD

The soul of the sluggard desireth, and hath nothing:
but the soul of the diligent shall be made fat.
Proverbs 13:4

TODD'S FEAR OF BAPTISM
WASN'T RATIONAL.

He will turn again, he will have compassion upon us;
he will subdue our iniquities; and thou wilt cast all
their sins into the depths of the sea. Micah 7:19

TEACHER'S PET

Pride goeth before destruction,
and an haughty spirit before a fall.
Proverbs 16:18

THE INSPECTOR COULDN'T QUITE PUT HIS
FINGER ON IT, BUT HE KNEW SOMETHING
FUNNY WAS GOING ON.

See then that ye walk circumspectly,
not as fools, but as wise.
Ephesians 5:15

"...AND UNTIL THIS DROUGHT IS OVER, WE'VE ASKED OUR BROTHER JOHN THE METHODIST HERE TO HANDLE ALL OUR BAPTISMS!"

One Lord, one faith, one baptism...
Ephesians 4:5

"DON'T TELL ME..."

The thing that hath been, it is that which shall be; and that which is done is that which shall be done: and there is no new thing under the sun. Eccl. 1:9

ABU WAS IN THE MIDDLE OF TELLING A JOKE WHEN
IT HAPPENED. HE REALLY HATED IT WHEN HE WAS
CUT OFF BEFORE HE GOT TO THE PUNCH LINE.

*Therefore is the name of it called Babel; because the
Lord did there confound the language of all the earth.*
Genesis 11:9

...we shall be satisfied with the goodness of thy house, even of thy holy temple.
Psalm 65:4b

CHILDREN COME TO TARZAN'S HOUSE.

Thy wife shall be as a fruitful vine by the sides of thine house: thy children like olive plants round about thy table. Psalm 128:3

Know ye not that they which run in a race run all, but one receiveth the prize? So run, that ye may obtain.
1 Corinthians 9:24

BANKER BOB WAS NO HYPOCRITE. HE WASN'T
ASHAMED TO SHOW HIS FAITH
AT HIS WORKPLACE.

*Whosoever therefore shall confess me before men, him
will I confess also before my Father which is in heaven.*
Matthew 10:32

AS MIKEY GOES UP FOR A SLAM DUNK, A CONTACT LENS POPS OUT, CAUSING A SLIGHT MISCALCULATION IN HIS AIM.

For he is cast into a net by his own feet,
and he walketh upon a snare.
Job 18:8

AFTER REPAIRING THE DAMAGE WITH STRIPS OF
LEAD, VINNIE LUCHESE HAD INVENTED THE
FIRST STAINED GLASS WINDOW.

For now we see through a glass, darkly; but then face to
face: now I know in part; but then shall I know even as
also I am known. 1 Corinthians 13:12

BECAUSE OF A STUPID CHILDHOOD
CURIOSITY, PEABODY WAS FORCED TO
EXTEND HIS STAY AMONG THE ESKIMOS.

Death and life are in the power of the tongue:
and they that love it shall eat the fruit thereof.
Proverbs 18:21

THE SHAKESPEAREAN ACTOR'S DILEMMA

Draw nigh to God, and he will draw nigh to you.
Cleanse your hands, ye sinners; and purify your hearts,
ye double minded. James 4:8

© 2004
JOE McCORMICK

MEN AND THEIR REMOTES...

A man's heart deviseth his way:
but the Lord directeth his steps.
Proverbs 16:9

"I JUST LOVE THOSE DROLL OBJECT LESSONS YOU
USE TO ILLUSTRATE YOUR SERMONS! I CAN'T
WAIT TO SEE WHAT SURPRISE YOU HAVE
IN STORE FOR US TODAY!"

For our God is a consuming fire.
Hebrews 12:29

"WAY I LOOK AT IT, IF OL' BUBBA CAN'T
BREAK THE WILD ONES, AT LEAST HE CAN
SPRAIN 'EM PRETTY BAD!"

*Wherefore seeing we also are compassed about with so
great a cloud of witnesses, let us lay aside every weight,
and the sin which doth so easily beset us...* Heb. 12:1

"HEY, I KNOW...LET'S SCATTER A FEW BAGS OF
SEASHELLS AND SHARKS' TEETH AROUND
UP HERE. SOME DAY IT'LL DRIVE
ARCHAEOLOGISTS NUTS!"

For they sleep not, except they have done mischief.
Proverbs 4:16

HAZEL WAS ALWAYS LATE FOR CHURCH...
BUT HER EXCUSES WERE AIRTIGHT.

...the spirit indeed is willing, but the flesh is weak.
Matthew 26:41

PETEY HAD PERFECTED THE ART OF BEGGING FOR TABLE SCRAPS.

I have been young, and now am old; yet have I not seen the righteous forsaken, nor his seed begging bread.
Psalm 37:25

"DISPATCH? LOOK, WE...HAHAHA...THERE'S A TRUCK
JACKNIFED ON I-40 AT...HEHEHE...IT'S A MESS...
YAHAHAHA...SEND A TOW TRUCK...HEE HEE
HEE...HAHAHA! NO, IT'S NOT AN APRIL FOOL JOKE,
IDIOT...HAHAHAHEEHEE..."

*I said of laughter, It is mad: and
of mirth, What doeth it?*
Ecclesiastes 2:2

"JOSHUA, WOULD YOU CUT THAT OUT AND COME ON?!"

*And he saith unto them, Follow me, and I
will make you fishers of men.*
Matthew 4:14

"I SWEAR THIS IS THE LAST TIME I LET THE KIDS INVITE COMPANY FOR LUNCH!"

The liberal soul shall be made fat:
and he that watereth shall be watered also himself.
Proverbs 11:25

"JACK LEG LAWYER!"

He that passeth by, and meddleth with strife belonging not to him, is like one that taketh a dog by the ears.
Proverbs 26:17

AFTER HE FOUND OUT HIS DONKEY
COULD TALK, BALAAM TRIED TO TRAIN
HIM AS A VENTRILOQUIST FOR
A TALKING DOG ACT.

*As a mad man who casteth firebrands, arrows, and
death, So is the man that deceiveth his neighbour, and
saith, Am not I in sport?* Proverbs 26:18-19

HAROLD WAS SLOWLY COMING TO GRIPS
WITH THE OBVIOUS. CLOTHES REALLY
DON'T MAKE THE MAN.

Do ye look on things after the outward appearance?
2 Corinthians 10:7

ARNOLD FINALLY REALIZED THAT IF HE
WAS EVER GOING TO MAKE SOMETHING OF HIMSELF,
HE'D HAVE TO GO AHEAD AND SPRING FOR THE
OTHER HALF OF THAT BODYBUILDING COURSE.

For the body is not one member, but many.
1 Corinthians 12:14

SAMSON HAD SEEN THIS VISION IN THE SKY
BEFORE. HE WONDERED WHAT IT MEANT.

*And it shall come to pass in the last days, saith God, I
will pour out of my Spirit upon all flesh...and your
young men shall see visions...* Acts 2:17

FIDO SUFFERED FROM A NERVOUS TICK.

And our hope of you is steadfast, knowing, that as ye are partakers of the sufferings, so shall ye be also of the consolation. 2 Corinthians 1:7

SOME PATENTS THAT DIDN'T MAKE IT.

Lo, this only have I found, that God hath made man upright; but they have sought out many inventions. Ecclesiastes 7:29

CARD GAMES ADAM PLAYED.

And the Lord God said, It is not good that the man should be alone; I will make him an help meet for him.
Genesis 2:18

JOE, THE HIGHROLLER, FINALLY TAKES HIS WIFE ON THE CRUISE HE ALWAYS PROMISED.

For all the promises of God in him are yea, and in him
Amen, unto the glory of God by us.
2 Corinthians 1:20

IF CLEM HADN'T BEEN EXPERIENCED AT READING THE SIGNS OF THE DESERT, HE'D NEVER HAVE SURVIVED.

When the poor and needy seek water, and there is none, and their tongue faileth for thirst, I the Lord will hear them, I the God of Israel will not forsake them. Isaiah 41:17

For the Lord himself shall descend from heaven with a shout…and with the trump of God: and the dead in Christ shall rise first. 1 Thessalonians 4:16

ZEKE KNEW THERE WERE NO FISH IN THE
BARREL, BUT IT SURE WAS MIGHTY HANDY.

Slothfulness casteth into a deep sleep;
and an idle soul shall suffer hunger.
Proverbs 13:15

© 2004

"I DUNNO...SOMETHING STINKS ABOUT THIS WHOLE THING!"

If the whole body were an eye, where were the hearing?
If the whole were hearing, where were the smelling?
1 Corinthians 12:17

JUSTINE'S UNCLE WAS RIGHT ABOUT WHAT WOULD HAPPEN IF HE EVER SET FOOT IN A CHURCH.

I was glad when they said unto me,
Let us go into the house of the Lord.
Psalm 122:1

EARLY SCRIBES AND THEIR TOOLS

For had ye believed Moses,
ye would have believed me: for he wrote of me.
John 5:46

"YOUR EPISTLE IS HERE!"

I charge you by the Lord that this epistle be
read unto all the holy brethren.
1Thessalonians 5:27

IN ONE OF THE LESSER KNOWN EVENTS OF
THE EXODUS FROM EGYPT, THE WORLD'S FIRST
FAST-FOOD JOINT SUFFERS A SWIFT
AND DRAMATIC DEMISE.

Man did eat angels' food...
Psalm 78:25

EXPLORING A WORM HOLE IN OUTER SPACE,
THE STARSHIP CREW MAKES A
SHOCKING DISCOVERY.

*Enter ye in at the strait gate: for wide is the gate, and
broad is the way, that leadeth to destruction...*
Matthew 7:13

IF THERE WAS ONE THING TINA KNEW, IT WAS WHEN IT WAS TIME TO GO OFF HER DIET.

Let your moderation be known
unto all men. The Lord is at hand.
Philippians 4:5

BUSINESS ENTERPRISES THAT
ADAM BRIEFLY CONSIDERED AND
QUICKLY DISCARDED

In the sweat of thy face shalt thou eat bread...
Genesis 3:19

"HEY, TED, CHECK THIS OUT. OUR MARS LANDER IS TRANSMITTING SOME NEW PICTURES YOU MIGHT FIND INTERESTING."

Be astonished, O ye heavens, at this, and be horribly afraid, be ye very desolate, saith the Lord.
Jeremiah 2:12

"HOW DO YOU THINK MOM FOUND OUT WE'D BEEN INTO THE BLACKBERRY JAM?"

...be sure your sin will find you out.
Numbers 32:23

FUTURE GENERATIONS WOULD WISH THE GARDEN HOE HAD BEEN INVENTED SOONER.

But of the tree of the knowledge of good and evil, thou shalt not eat of it: for in the day that thou eatest thereof thou shalt surely die. Genesis 2:17

HOW STUFF GETS STARTED DEPT.

"OH, GOODY, YOU'RE HOME! WOULD YOU GIVE ME A HAND WITH THIS SOFA, ATTILA HON?"

Who is a wise man and endued with knowledge among you? let him shew out of a good conversation his works with meekness of wisdom. James 3:13

© 2004

"IF THE STEAK IS TOO TOUGH, WHY DON'T YOU JUST SAY SO?"

Likewise, ye husbands, dwell with them according to knowledge, giving honour unto the wife...
1 Peter 3:7

HIDDEN HIGH IN THE BALCONY, AT THE END OF THE PASTOR'S SPELLBINDING SERMON ON THE END TIMES, ARTY PREPARES TO EMPTY THE CHURCH.

For the Lord himself shall descend from heaven with a shout, with the voice of the archangel, and with the trump of God. 1 Thessalonians 4:16

MONDAY WAS SYLVIA'S DAY TO GET
UP ON THE WRONG SIDE OF THE BED.

The discretion of a man deferreth his anger; and it is
his glory to pass over a transgression.
Proverbs 19:11

CLIFFORD REALIZES TOO LATE THAT HE WAS FLYING A TAD TOO HIGH TO USE THE EJECTION SEAT.

All we like sheep have gone astray; we have turned every one to his own way; and the Lord hath laid on him the iniquity of us all. Isaiah 53:6

"I HOPE DEACON SMITH DOESN'T BORE
US TO DEATH TALKING ABOUT HIS CHILDREN.
ACCORDING TO HIM, THEY'RE THE MOST
UNUSUAL KIDS IN THE WORLD!"

*My brethren, have not the faith of our Lord Jesus
Christ, the Lord of glory, with respect of persons.*
James 2:1

"WAIT! DON'T ANYBODY EAT THAT
SALAD UNTIL WE FIND OUT WHAT THE
TRANSPORTER DID WITH SCOTTY!"

*It is good neither to eat flesh, nor to drink wine, nor any
thing whereby thy brother stumbleth, or is offended, or
is made weak.* Romans 14:21

ALFREDO FINALLY WAS FORCED
TO ADMIT THAT HIS COACH WAS RIGHT...
HE JUST DIDN'T HAVE THE BUILD
TO BE A POLE VAULTER.

*For which of you, intending to build a tower, sitteth not
down first, and counteth the cost...*
Luke 14:28

"MAMA, JOEY DID SOMETHING JESUS WOULDN'T DO!"

For nothing is secret, that shall not be made manifest; neither any thing hid, that shall not be known and come abroad. Luke 8:17

THIS FAMILIAR, TIME-HONORED ENCOURAGEMENT
TO ACTORS FIRST ORIGINATED IN 1611 WHEN
NOTED BONE SURGEON PHINEAS E. DOUGAL
SENT BEST WISHES TO THE CAST OF
"TAMING OF THE SHREW."

Faithful are the wounds of a friend...
Proverbs 27:6

"HE ALWAYS BRAGGED HE COULD DO THE TEN YEARS STANDING ON HIS HEAD!"

For it is better, if the will of God be so, that ye suffer for well doing, than for evil doing.
1 Peter 3:17

"WHOAH! LOOKS LIKE THE COMPETITION DOWN
THERE TO HAVE THE TALLEST STEEPLE
IS GETTING OUT OF HAND!"

Except the Lord build the house,
they labour in vain that build it...
Psalm 127:1

COFFEE IN HAND, SUPPLIES AT THE READY,
ALICE SETTLES IN, WAITING FOR THE
FIRST TELEMARKETER TO CALL.

Judgments are prepared for scorners,
and stripes for the back of fools.
Proverbs 19:29

"IT'S GOING TO BE A LONG DAY!"

For this cause shall a man leave his father and mother, and shall be joined unto his wife, and they two shall be one flesh. Ephesians 5:31

"YOU BORROWED HOW MUCH TO FINANCE THIS THING? NOAH, DO YOU REALIZE HOW MANY YEARS IT WILL TAKE TO PAY THAT BACK?"

Owe no man any thing, but to love one another: for he that loveth another hath fulfilled the law.
Romans 13:8

IT CAUSED ARTURO NO END OF EMBARRASSMENT
WHEN HIS MOBSTER BROTHER BORROWED HIS
VIOLIN CASE AND DIDN'T PUT THINGS
BACK LIKE THEY WERE.

...And they were astonished with a great astonishment.
Mark 5:42

EARL HAD LIVED A FULL LIFE. HE PARTIED
EVERY NIGHT, DRANK LIKE A FISH, SMOKED
FOUR PACKS A DAY. HERE WE SEE EARL
CELEBRATING HIS 24TH BIRTHDAY.

Let us walk honestly, as in the day; not in rioting and
drunkenness, not in chambering and wantonness...
Romans 13:13

LEROY WASN'T SURE WHY HE WAS SUPPOSED
TO GO TO THE ANT, BUT, WELL...HE
READ IT IN THE BIBLE.

Go to the ant, thou sluggard;
consider her ways, and be wise.
Proverbs 6:6

TAP DANCER'S NIGHTMARE

Be ye angry, and sin not:
let not the sun go down upon your wrath.
Ephesians 4:26

"HONEY...DO YOU THINK WE'RE LETTING
JIMMY WATCH TOO MUCH TV?"

*Lo, children are an heritage of the Lord:
and the fruit of the womb is his reward.*
Psalm 127:3

LITTLE NOAH'S SAVINGS PLAN

*But my God shall supply all your need
according to his riches in glory by Christ Jesus.*
Philippians 4:19

HAVING BLOWN THE MONEY FOR
PAINTING THE SISTINE CHAPEL CEILING PRETTY
QUICKLY, MICHELANGELO MAKES
A DEAL FOR THE FLOOR.

The glory of this latter house shall be greater
than of the former, saith the Lord of hosts...
Haggai 2:9

NOBODY WAS BUYING VINCENT'S PAINTINGS.
HE GAVE SOME THOUGHT TO TAKING UP A CAREER
IN MUSIC, BUT REALIZED HE REALLY
DIDN'T HAVE AN EAR FOR IT.

*As every man hath received the gift, even so minister
the same one to another, as good stewards of the
manifold grace of God.* 1Peter 4:10

"OKAY, GANG...WE'LL TAKE FIVE
WHILE CLAUDE GETS THE FROG
OUT OF HIS THROAT!"

But the Lord is in his holy temple:
let all the earth keep silence before him.
Habakkuk 2:20

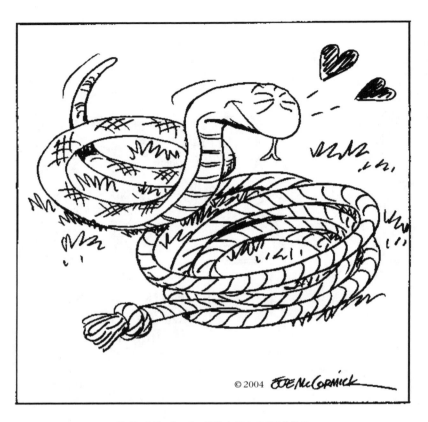

LOVE AT NEAR SIGHT

Then the eyes of the blind shall be opened,
and the ears of the deaf shall be unstopped.
Isaiah 35:5

LENNY WAS THE STAR PLAYER, BUT HIS
TEAM LOST THE GAME WHILE HE WAS
PUTTING ON HIS SHOES.

*And your feet shod with the preparation
of the gospel of peace.*
Ephesians 6:15

"HONEY, YOU SHOULDN'T DO THAT.
YOUR FATHER'S NERVES ARE STRETCHED
RATHER THIN SINGE HE TOOK OVER
CHILDREN'S CHURCH!"

For whom the Lord loveth he correcteth;
even as a father the son in whom he delighteth.
Proverbs 3:12

UNDER CERTAIN CONDITIONS ROGER COULD
OVERCOME HIS FEAR OF HEIGHTS.

...but the people that do know their
God shall be strong, and do exploits.
Daniel 11:32

AT FIRST, ARTISTS DIDN'T DO WELL IN THE WEST.
THEY TENDED TO MISUNDERSTAND WHEN A BAD
GUY STEPPED OUT OF A SALOON AND YELLED,
"DRAW, PILGRIM!"

...be not children in understanding.
1 Corinthians 14:20

"HE MAY NOT BE A DYNAMIC PREACHER, BUT YOU HAVE TO ADMIT HE KNOWS HOW TO KEEP AN AUDIENCE AWAKE!"

For after that in the wisdom of God the world by wisdom knew not God, it pleased God by the foolishness of preaching to save them that believe. 1 Cor. 1:21

"LET'S SEE...WHAT SHOULD WE NAME HIM?"

...and whatsoever Adam called every living
creature, that was the name thereof.
Genesis 2:19

"I'VE GOT A TAIL LIGHT OUT? WHOA, MAN, WHAT
A RELIEF! I THOUGHT YOU WERE STOPPING ME
BECAUSE OF THE DRUGS STASHED IN THE
POCKETS OF THE DEAD GUY IN THE TRUNK!"

*...for out of the abundance of the heart
the mouth speaketh.*
Matthew 12:34

"IF THIS GUY OFFERS US ANY FISHING
ADVICE, I SUGGEST WE TAKE IT!"

Hear instruction, and be wise, and refuse it not.
Proverbs 8:33

FREDDIE REMINGTON'S MOM WANTED TO SHOW HER
SUPPORT FOR HIS DECISION TO GO WEST TO
PAINT. SHE SENT HIM A BOX OF SUPPLIES.

*Arise; for this matter belongeth unto thee: we also
will be with thee: be of good courage, and do it.*
Ezra 10:4

"PETE? GET THE BOSS ON THE LINE, WILL YOU? WE'VE GOT A PROBLEM HERE!"

Trust in the Lord with all thine heart; and lean not unto thine own understanding In all thy ways acknowledge him, and he shall direct thy paths.
Proverbs 3:5-6

"GOLD? WHY WOULD YOU WANT TO BRING A
SACK OF PAVEMENT INTO HEAVEN?"

*...and the street of the city was pure gold,
as it were transparent glass.*
Revelation 21:21

WHEN ANTS WATCH TOO MUCH T.V.

They compassed me about; yea, they compassed me about: but in the name of the Lord I will destroy them.
Psalm 118:11

DENKINS HAD BEEN A ROOKIE FOR
MORE THAN A MONTH BEFORE THEY LET HIM
GRILL A SUSPECT. HE WAS EAGER TO
LEARN HOW IT WAS DONE.

The preparations of the heart in man,
and the answer of the tongue, is from the Lord.
Proverbs 16:1

CARD GAMES ABOARD THE ARK

There went in two and two unto Noah into the ark, the
male and the female, as God had commanded Noah.
Genesis 7:9

"MY DAD CAN LICK YOUR DAD!"

But the tongue can no man tame;
it is an unruly evil, full of deadly poison.
James 3:8

ELMER'S MOTHER HAD BEEN RIGHT. HE WASN'T
WEARING CLEAN UNDERWEAR THE NIGHT OF THE
TORNADO AND THE EMT'S WOULDN'T TOUCH HIM.

*Honour thy father and thy mother, as the Lord thy God
hath commanded thee; that thy days may be prolonged,
and that it may go well with thee.* Deuteronomy 5:16

"YOU WON'T FIND ANY DUST ON MY BIBLE, PASTOR. I HAD IT SHRINK-WRAPPED TO PROTECT IT!"

Blessed is he that readeth, and they that hear the words of this prophecy, and keep those things which are written therein... Revelation 1:3

"DAD, I'M 65 AND YOU'RE 87. DON'T YOU THINK
IT'S TIME WE FOUND ANOTHER NAME
FOR ME BESIDES 'BOY'?"

*Thou shalt rise up before the hoary head, and honour
the face of the old man, and fear thy God: I am the Lord.*
Leviticus 19:32

"DO YOU HAVE ANY BUSHES
WITHOUT DEVILS BEHIND THEM?"

Behold, I give unto you power to tread on serpents and scorpions, and over all the power of the enemy: and nothing shall by any means hurt you. Luke 10:19

"YOU SAY THAT YOU KEEP HEARING
YOUR NAME CALLED FROM THE SKY? TELL ME...
HOW CLOSE DO YOU LIVE TO THE
NEW SKYDIVING SCHOOL?"

*Unto you, O men, I call; and my voice
is to the sons of man.*
Proverbs 8:4

THE NIGHT DEACON JONES
SPOKE IN TONGUES

And that, knowing the time, that now it is high time to awake out of sleep: for now is our salvation nearer than when we believed. Romans 13:11

DR. JIM'S LITTLE DENTIST JOKE BACKFIRES

And he saith unto them, Why are ye
fearful, O ye of little faith?
Matthew 8:26

"NO, IT REALLY ISN'T A MIRACLE. HE
THOUGHT HE SAW A WATER MOCCASIN!"

How can a man that is a sinner do such miracles?
John 9:16

"OMIGOSH! IT'S THE GUY WHO MODELS FOR
PICASSO! WHERE DO WE EVEN START
TO TAKE A BLOOD PRESSURE?"

And Jesus answering said unto them, They that are
whole need not a physician; but they that are sick.
Luke 5:31

"SOMETHING TELLS ME HE PLANS TO STEP ON SOMEBODY'S TOES TONIGHT!"

When Jesus knew in himself that his disciples murmured at it, he said unto them, Doth this offend you?
John 6:61

"IT'S HARD TO DESCRIBE, DOC. I JUST DON'T KNOW IF I'M COMING OR GOING ANYMORE!"

I am full of confusion;
therefore see thou mine affliction...
Job 10:15

MOSES DIDN'T THINK HIS GRANDMA WOULD
EVER MAKE IT AS AN ARTIST, BUT IT
GAVE HER SOMETHING TO DO...

*And even to your old age I am he; and even to hoar
hairs will I carry you: I have made, and I will bear;
even I will carry, and will deliver you.* Isaiah 46:4

"WHEN DID YOU FIRST NOTICE THAT YOUR

*Therefore I say unto you, Take no thought
for your life, what ye shall eat,*

144

© 2004
JOE McCORMICK

PROBLEMS WERE GETTING TOO BIG FOR YOU?"

*or what ye shall drink; nor yet for your body,
what ye shall put on?* Matthew 6:25

OXYMORONS OF THE WEST

For my yoke is easy, and my burden is light.
Matthew 11:30

SOME OF THE WAYS GOD SPEAKS TO MAN...
GOT YOUR EARS ON?

O earth, earth, earth, hear the word of the Lord.
Jeremiah 22:29

ABOUT THE AUTHOR

Joe McCormick was born in rural West Tennessee, received his art training in Southern California, and began his career in a Memphis advertising agency. He does commercial illustrations and cartoons for a wide variety of clients across the United States. The artist also paints wildlife, landscapes and portraits, and enjoys photography, writing and travel.

Joe lives in Pinson, Tennessee with his wife Beverly, who is a registered nurse. The McCormicks have been involved in mission work for the past twenty years, having served first with Wycliffe Bible Translators. They are currently affiliated with International Gospel Outreach of Semmes, Alabama.

To contact the author write:
Joe McCormick
676 Cedarfield Road
Pinson, TN 38366